STATUES OF LIMITATIONS

STATUES

OF LIMITATIONS

INTIMATE VIEWS OF LIFE AMONG THE MARBLES

by DENISON HATCH

COWARD-McCANN, Inc.   NEW YORK

STATUES OF LIMITATIONS

"Mr. Johnson, do you remember that salesman you couldn't bear to fire?"

PERSEUS
Cellini
Loggia dei Lanzi, Florence

"When Jimmy say it's time to strike, it's time to strike!"

GREEK COMIC ACTOR
Museum of Fine Arts, Boston

ST. GEORGE
Fremiet
Luxembourg, Paris

"This will teach you not to beg at the table!"

"Better put a quart in anyway to be on the safe side."

SCIENCE
Giovanni da Bologna
Genoa

"This will teach you not to beg at the table!"

"Better put a quart in anyway to be on the safe side."

SCIENCE
Giovanni da Bologna
Genoa

"We were made for each other."

THE KISS
Brancusi
Philadelphia Museum of Art

NYMPH AND SATYR
Clodion
Metropolitan Museum, New York

"It's Brylcreem, honey — just a few dabs for your hair."

"Now, Miss White, you've called in sick the last three Mondays."

MENANDER
Vatican

"Surely not mousse au chocolat after crepes suzette, Mrs. Kennedy."

GABRIELE FONSECA
Bernini
Fonseca Chapel, Rome

*"Who had the bright idea
to go skin diving?"*

EROS ENTWINED BY DOLPHIN
Naples

"If that's Boots and Saddles, *I'm Man O'War."*

TRUMPETER
Meissonier
Luxembourg, Paris

"Sylvia, where the hell's the light cord?"

DANCING FAUN
National Museum, Naples
Photo Alinari

GODDESS OF THE BIRDS
Louvre, Paris

"The House of Dior hasn't been the same since they got rid of St. Laurent."

"Gadge wants it this way."

THE THREE SHADOWS
Rodin

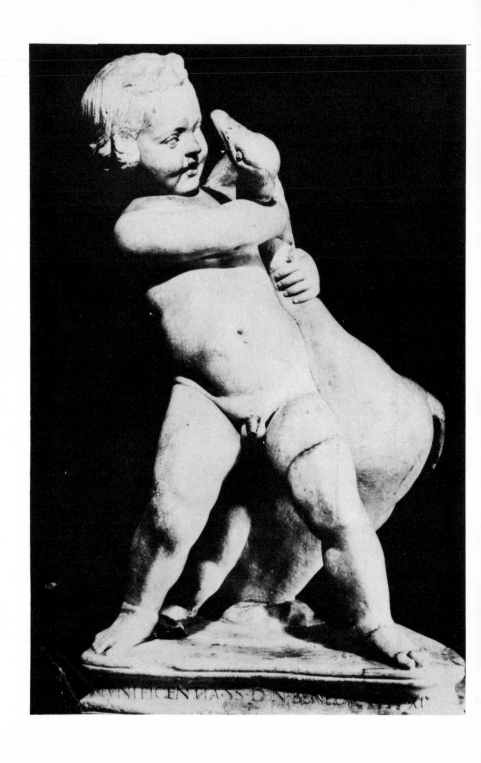

"Take me to your Leda."

BOY WITH WATERFOWL
Boethus
Capitoline Museum, Rome

HEAD OF CYCLADIC IDOL
Louvre, Paris

"Marry into royalty, and you lose your identity."

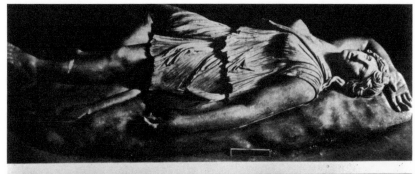

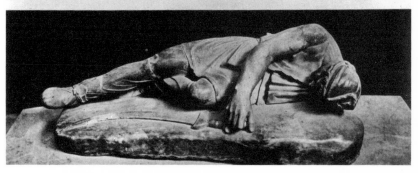

"City living is almost bearable with a terrace."

DEAD AMAZON; DEAD GAUL;
DEAD PERSIAN
National Museum, Naples

"Chrysler down another two points. Damn! Damn! DAMN!"

MARSYAS
Myron
Lateran Museum, Rome
Photo Alinari

MVNIFICENTIA PII·IX·PONT·MAX

HEAD OF ALKYONEUS
Pergamon Altar
Pergamon Museum, Berlin

"What's the best thing for a hangover?"

SERVANT GIRL FROM TOMB
Berlin

"Go on, tell me some more of the cute things Tony did before I married him."

"It's no use. We'll have to get a stepladder."

RAPE OF THE SABINE
Giovanni da Bologna
Naples

"So you want to break up housekeeping, do you?"

DISCUS THROWER of Castel
Porzioano (after Myron)
Terme, Rome
Photo Alinari

NYMPH by Calamech
NEPTUNE by Ammanati
Fountain, Piazzi della Signoria,
Florence

"Don't look now, but isn't that Maria and Ari doing the pachanga?"

"You must have hit these into our court."

VENUS GENETRIX
Louvre, Paris
Photo Giraudon

"Sorry my partner couldn't be here — but, then, he's the inside man."

HORSE
Acropolis Museum, Athens

"We'd love to stay longer, but he has to work tomorrow."

GLORIA VICTIS
Mercié

VENUS
Canova
Pitti Gallery, Florence

"Damn it, Philip! Can't you ask them to wait in the main salon?"

DYING WARRIOR
Munich

*"Now remember — don't blow the hatch off until you
see the helicopters."*

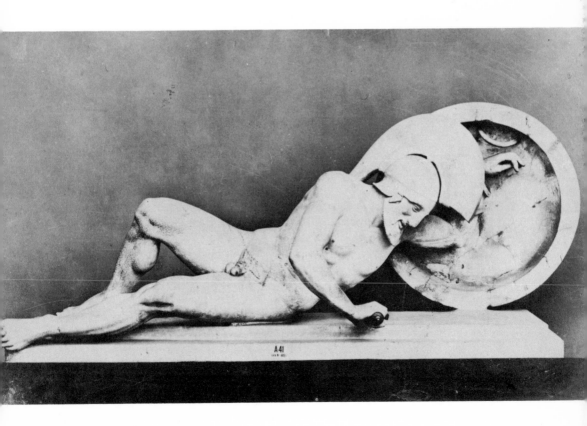

Only her hairdresser knows . . .

WOMAN COMBING HER HAIR
Archipenko
Collection Museum of Modern Art,
New York

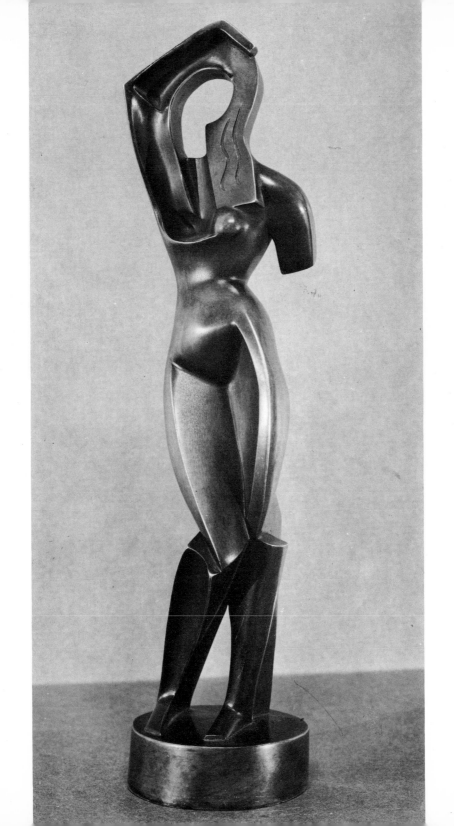

"Hey, Romulus! This one's chocolate!"

WOLF OF THE CAPITOLINE
Palazzo dei Conservatori, Rome
Photo Alinari

"Girls, this is Edgar. We've half decided to run off and get married."

TWO EGYPTIANS
Louvre, Paris
Photo Giraudon

"Usually I never kiss a boy on the first date."

THE KISS
Rodin

DIONYSUS
From the Parthenon
British Museum, London

"And then Comrade Khrushchev said, 'I never bite the hand that feeds me.'"

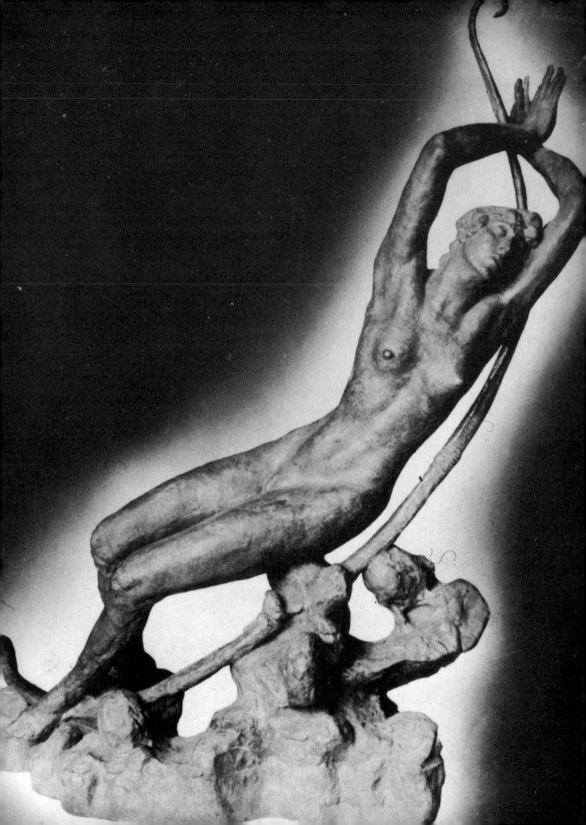

"Is this really how Marilyn got started?"

SELENE
Bourdelle
Vassar College, New York

"That was a beautiful swan dive, Mr. Thomas. Now let's find our clothes and get back to the party."

"Since when don't you eat grapefruit?"

POETESS
Palazzo dei Conservatori, Rome

"So this is a quiet weekend at Glen Ora!"

BATTLE
Giovanni da Bertoldo
Bargello, Florence

"Gosh, you have a cold nose!"

DEER WITH FAWN
Museum of Fine Arts, Boston

"But, doctor, I just want my ears pierced."

APHRODITE ANADYOMENE
Vatican

"You should have seen me before I went to Vic Tanny's."

STANDING WOMAN
Lachaise
Collection Museum of Modern Art,
New York

"Harry, shut the damn window."

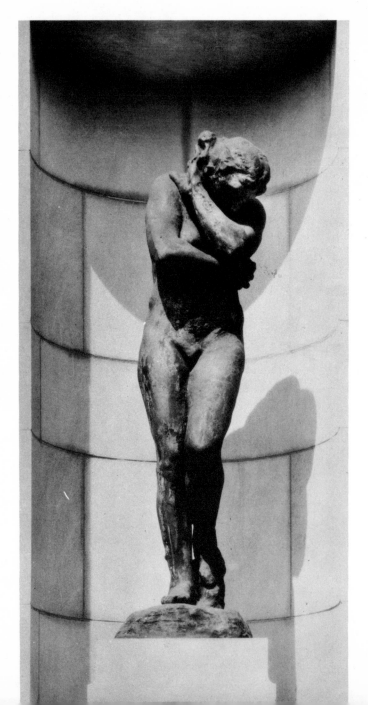

EVE
Rodin
Rodin Museum,
Philadelphia

*"You must realize, Miss Gompers, that if JFK limits
expense accounts, all this must end."*

RECLINING FIGURE from
Etruscan Sarcophagus
National Museum, Florence

"Oscar, is there a shine on my nose again?"

WALKING WOMAN
Lachaise
Private Collection, New York

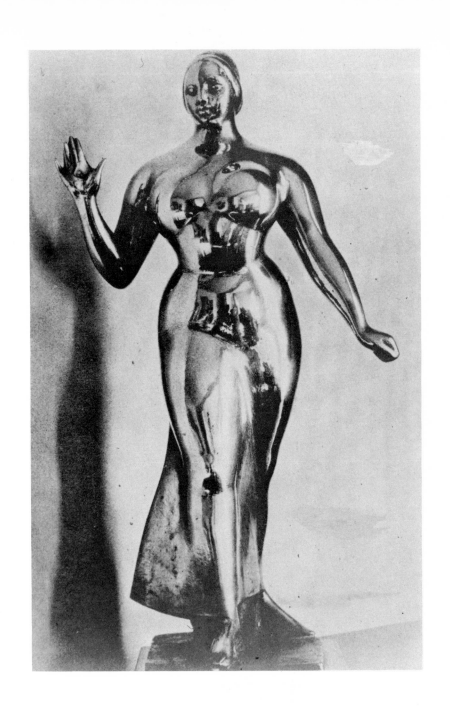

"Do you think it's too sheer?"

APHRODITE
British Museum, London

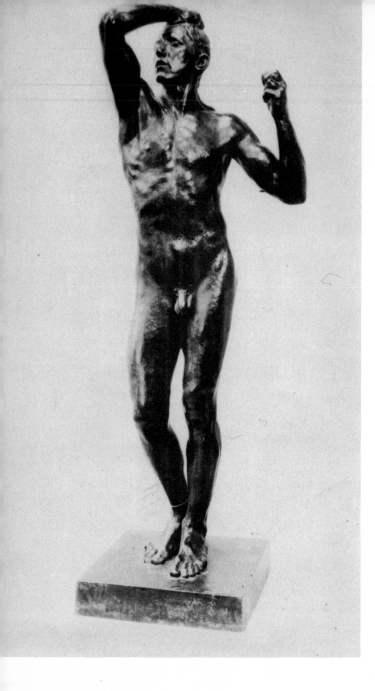

AGE OF BRONZE
Rodin

"Honestly, Meg, I get so sick of always having to bow down to that sister of yours."

"The old man says the mink is yours if you'll just lay off his imported sherry."

BACCHANTE
MacMonnies
Metropolitan Museum, New York

The bitter end . . .

MILO OF CROTON
Puget
Louvre, Paris